M000188421

TRANSMITTER AND RECEIVER

Transmitter and Receiver

Raoul Fernandes

NIGHTWOOD EDITIONS | 2015

Copyright © Raoul Fernandes, 2015

ALL RIGHTS RESERVED. No part of this publication may be reproduced, stored in a retrieval system or transmitted, in any form or by any means, without prior permission of the publisher or, in the case of photocopying or other reprographic copying, a licence from Access Copyright, the Canadian Copyright Licensing Agency, www.accesscopyright.ca, info@accesscopyright.ca.

Nightwood Editions
P.O. Box 1779
Gibsons, BC VON 1VO
Canada
www.nightwoodeditions.com

TYPOGRAPHY & DESIGN: Carleton Wilson

Nightwood Editions acknowledges financial support from the Government of Canada through the Canada Book Fund and the Canada Council for the Arts, and from the Province of British Columbia through the British Columbia Arts Council and the Book Publisher's Tax Credit.

This book has been produced on 100% post-consumer recycled, ancient-forest-free paper, processed chlorine-free and printed with vegetable-based dyes.

Printed and bound in Canada.

LIBRARY AND ARCHIVES CANADA CATALOGUING IN PUBLICATION

Fernandes, Raoul, 1978-, author
Transmitter and receiver : poems / by Raoul Fernandes.

Poems.
Issued in print and electronic formats.
ISBN 978-0-88971-309-3 (pbk.).--ISBN 978-0-88971-046-7 (pdf)

I. Title.

PS8611.E749T73 2015   C811'.6   C2015-901128-0
                                              C2015-901129-9

For Megan

CONTENTS

1

2

3

BY WAY OF EXPLANATION

You have this thing you can only explain
by driving me out to the port at night
to watch the towering cranes moving containers
from ship to train. Or we go skipping stones
across the mirror of the lake, a ghost ship
in a bottle of blue Bombay gin by your side.
I have this thing I can only explain to you
by showing you a pile of computer hardware
chucked into the ravine. We hike down there
and blackberry vines grab our clothes as if to say,
Stop, wait, I want to tell you something too.
You have an old photograph you keep in your
bedside drawer. I have this song I learned
on my guitar. By way of clarification, you send
me a YouTube video of a tornado filmed up close
from a parked car. Or a live-stream from a public
camera whose view is obscured by red leaves.
I cut you a key to this room, this door.
There's this thing. A dictionary being consumed
by fire. The two of us standing in front of a Rothko
until time starts again. A mixtape that is primarily
about the clicks and hums between songs. What if
we walk there instead of driving? What if we just drive,
without a destination? There's this thing I've always
wanted to talk about with someone. Now
with you here, with you listening, with all
the antennae raised, I no longer have to.

Permission to use that snowball
you've been keeping in the freezer
since 1998. For a poem? she asks.
What else? I say. I'll trade you, she says
for that thing your mom said
at the park. What was it?
"God, that mallard's being a real douchebag"?
Yes, that one. Deal, I say. Okay, how about
the Korean boy who walks past
our house late at night, singing
"Moon River"? Oh, you can use that, I say,
I wouldn't even know what
to do with it. But there is something else.
I've been wanting to write about
the black skirt we've been using to cover
the lovebird's cage. The goodnight skirt.
In exchange, I'll let you have
our drunken mailman, the tailless tabby,
and I'll throw in the broken grandfather clock
we found in the forest. One more, she says.
Last night, I say. The whole night.

She considers for a while, then,
Okay, that's fair. But I really had something going
with that lovebird. All right, I say, write it
anyway. If it's more beautiful than mine,
it's yours.

Walking through the sensor gate at the public library
after a heavy reading, you fear the alarm
will go off from what is held in your mind.
You reassure yourself with the thought that no matter
how fuzzy it gets in the wire-tangled AV room,
you are still lunch, with possible leftovers,
for that wolf and her cubs. You have to imagine
the wolf and her cubs, obviously, but it helps.
When it comes down to it, it's completely dark
just a few millimetres beneath the skin, no matter
how real the flickers on your nerve endings feel,
what with this strong coffee, this pulsing sky. You remind
yourself deep-sea life forms have evolved bioluminescence
for practical, not spiritual, reasons. Lunch, leftovers, etc.
Wooden chairs are real and tangible,
which is why philosophers and poets are always
referring to them, holding onto them, when hovering
around their rooms. Sometimes you catch yourself
singing without knowing you are singing
and sometimes you don't even catch yourself.

The spine's threads and glue coming apart
from frequent shelving, being shoved into backpacks,
tossed across rooms; the cover tarnished,
water/coffee/wine damage,
dog ears, rippled pages, stains from a petal
pressed between pages 26 and 27,
tiny crushed insects like misplaced punctuation,
damage from the book louse's
feeding on the mould in the paper,
the mould too, of course, scribbled notes,
shards of highlighter, the slow fading
from light itself. Our fingerprints,
the oil of our hands, the oil and sweat
of our shaking, paper-cut hands.

You need a flashlight to find the flashlight.
A cup of coffee to muster the energy
to get to the coffee maker. Call
the phone-repair man with your smashed
phone. Decipher the patterns in the ceiling.
The pill that takes away your fear of heights
is at the top of the ladder. *I gave up everything for you,*
he says. *Everything that I wanted you to keep,*
she says. Signing up for the fire-juggling course
requires that you have already taken
the fire-juggling course. Your face hovering
above the puzzle is an unfinished puzzle. Scattered
sky-blue pieces. A frown is a frozen ripple.
A shudder is you trying to be in two places at once.
But there's a hole in the bucket, dear Liza, dear Liza.
Try and try, give up and try again. And give up.
I cannot say sorry until you say sorry first,
they both think. The oars to your boat are floating away.
Itch in the phantom limb. Cut flowers in the vase
with all their love-me/love-me-not petals.
You first, they both think. *Please.* You search
your pockets outside your locked car. Where
are they? Oh, right. In the ignition.
There they are.

The fast-cash ATM wonders why
        the woman looks so sad
when it prints out

pale numbers
        on a small piece of paper

after she clearly pressed yes
                when offered a receipt

wonders if this is some
        personal narrative
it is not privy to

through its built-in camera
        the ATM's limited view

is the lower half
of a streetlight pole

a newspaper box
                updated daily

        a laundromat across
the road with lopsided
hanging fluorescent lights

I'd print something better
if I could
                it thinks

fortune-cookie ribbons
          or
the inverse
     of every news headline

I'd generate some music
if I had more
     than one tone

crush that little paper
     it wants to say

          throw it into the air
behind you

from these winter blossoms
     our city will know

something better has to be
     dreamed up

               go along now
          there is another waiting
behind you

clutching his coat
     in all this
     cold swirling data

dreaming something too

Playground with interlocking tunnels. Willows worry
their reflections in the frog pond. Little gods throw spheres,
miss as often as they catch. Coins flicker in the fountain bed,
worth exactly the feeling of wishing. Leaves in circulation.
Runners in circulation. A young girl in the shade scratches
at a scratch-and-win. Grown men with dream journals in their
back pockets wander among the birch trees. Dolphin on a spring.
Rabbit on a spring. Swings used in inventive ways. Sweethearts.
A tall woman walks an oracular greyhound. A beetle-child
hums his way home from his cello lesson. Some bright flapping
memory is caught in a tree and is also an actual thing: a kite.
What happens in real life is absorbed into dream journals.
Flocks of young soccer players aligning, dispersing. A small
god pops an empty juice box under his sneaker. Another
laughs and shouts, *Angel! Angel!* as his dog pulls him
by the leash through a flowerbed. Frisbee-sliced air.
Pale moon on a string. A maple drops a leaf into your hair
to get your attention. Okay, sweetheart, you've got it.
Then more leaves drift down toward the earth.

BLACKOUT

The storm gathers, stirs a tree, breaks
a branch, takes out a cable, cuts the power,
quiets our fridge, watches us through the window
where we sit to eat ice cream in the dark.
You strike a match, cup the flame,
touch it to the candle's wick.
The city is already motioning to repair
but we can't hear it for the trees. We hope
it will take its time. Who will sit
at the piano tonight? The child
given relief from her homework. A relief
for the moment. The storm
raining its applause on the roof.

THIRTEEN SUMMERS FOR TIMOTHY TREADWELL
after the Werner Herzog documentary Grizzly Man

Out in Grizzly country, Timothy Treadwell films
a bumblebee sitting motionless on a stalk of fireweed,
believes the bee has expired with its head inside a flower,
its legs heavy with pollen. *It's beautiful, it's sad, it's tragic,*
he says in a breathless small-town-movie-theatre-cashier voice.

He steadies the camera on the fireweed, thinks
about that line in a song: *Lord let me die*
with a hammer in my hand.

I love that bee, he says.

The tapes contain hours of footage. There he is
resting his hand on some warm bear scat.
It came from inside her, he says. *It was just inside her.*

There he is screaming for rain during a drought,
when the salmon aren't running and the bears
are eating their own children.

Timothy films himself
holding a bear cub's skull.

Lord let me die
with my head inside a flower.

He looks into the holes where the cub's eyes would be.
Looks away much too soon.

When the bee moves Tim realizes
it was just sleeping. Days later, a bear paws honey
from Tim's chest. He is moaning, his girlfriend
screaming. The camera covers its eyes.

Love disperses like light
across the Alaskan wilderness.

You were depressed. There were more birds
in the yard.

Rising from the chair was difficult. The yard
was overgrown.

The lawnmower was in the shed. The weeds
were flowering.

You couldn't get to the lawnmower. The grass
was as tall as your shoulders.

You were unable to summon the strength. The yard
was audible with insects.

You touched the windowpane's glass. The outside world
thrummed with hidden creatures.

You were depressed. There were swallows, finches,
flickers and wrens.

THE TULIP VENDING MACHINE

An artificial sun over rows of tulips,
a scheduled rain that mists
the garden.

You put a coin in a slot, a blade
curves out, lops
a flower near the base
of its stem

and sometimes
if the stems are too close
or blade slightly off
it accidentally cuts two—this

is what moves you, how the flaw
makes the machine seem organic,
time-distressed, human.

And you are moved by
its other mistake—the blade slices
against a stem that isn't there,
the trap door opens,
the absence of a tulip falls
into the tray below,

and you reach your hand in
to collect it.

THE NEWSPAPER ARRIVES ALREADY PAPIER-MÂCHÉD INTO A VOLCANO

Someone potentially dangerous is released
to live and walk around your city. You take
a few moments to memorize the face
in the newspaper so it is not surprising
when the face appears in a dream
but treats you kindly: mops your brow,
brings you tea, slices a pear
the way you do.

The dream transitions, projects other images:
a river made of light bulbs smashing
against rocks, a pair of sneakers
hanging from power lines.

If you keep talking about dreams
all the eyes in the room will glaze over
and project better cinema
on their screens. There is better cinema:

webcam of baby eagles picking apart a rabbit
in a nest on a high cliff

or grainy figures walking in and out of banks
or lobbies of hotels.

You could watch them for hours
until your skin begins to flicker
and pixelate.

You could widen the aperture,
be taken by the river. Wear the shoes that hang
from the wire, walk lifetimes in them.

You arise from the dream, potentially dangerous
and released into your own home. Keep yourself
from glancing at your mirror or your kitchen knives
while you make coffee, feed your cat, collect
a newspaper full of faces, one morning,
all of them yours, a newspaper
you can't bear to open.

ONE EARLY MORNING...

for Ray and Kalindy

you wake up bed-headed and somewhere
in that tangle of hair is the signature
of the one beside you. Walk
across your kitchen floor thinking:
this tile pattern would go on forever if we didn't
put up some walls, a roof, a table, a vase
with some cut flowers.

Small garden-muddy footprints run over the floors,
up the walls, across the ceiling. The children
re-enact the stories you read them to sleep.
You make a promise without words. A secret handshake
you could share even if bound up in straitjackets.

Love poems composed on cutting boards,
in hot skillets. A fan above the oven that blows
the fragrant spices out into the neighbourhood.
Squirrels, crows, lovers, raccoons nod their heads,
breathe deep. You make a promise
beyond words. You cut a key
to hidden chambers. A key on your ring
that rings when tossed in the air
and caught.

*

A key being a small sentence. A lock wants to hear
only one thing. *Good*, says the key. *Morning*,
says the lock. *Bird*, says the key. *Cage*, says the lock.
Home, says the key. *Work*, says the lock. *Time*, says
the key. *Travel*, says the lock. *I like this game*, says the key.
Give me your name, says the lock. *Well*, says the key. *Spring*,
says the lock. *Gift*, says the key. *Wrap*, says the lock.
Water, says the key. *Fall*, says the lock. *We could do this all day*,
says the key. *It may well turn out that way*, says the lock.
Round, says the key. *About*, says the lock. *Tooth*, says the key.
Ache, says the lock. *Head*, says the key. *Ache*, says the lock.
Heart, says the key. *Ache*, says the lock. *Good*, says the key.
Night, says the lock. *Sweet*, says the key. *Dreams*, says the lock.
This is what I bring, says the key. *I only want to hear
one thing.*

(LOOP)

believe it. Saturn, ringed for centuries by
her own shattered moon, nowhere she can look

without seeing it. How often she tries

to will off her own gravity, send the pieces out
into the dark elsewhere. But knows

she can't or won't. What becomes
her halo, prayer-wheel, memory-laden hula hoop.
Spell-spun, perpetually dizzy. Some early morning

a neighbour coasts by, says, *Beautiful day*
and it takes all she can to look around her and

or a bracket or a latch
or a joint or a lock or a nut or a bolt
or a fastener or a buckle or a button or a hitch
or a nail or a screw or a toggle or a clamp
or a snap-ring or a dowel
or a lashing or a string or a zipper or a belt
or an anchor or a leash
or a dab of glue or a piece of sticky tape
or a staple or a strip of Velcro or a pair of jumper cables
or a router or the reins of a horse
or the stem of a hanging fruit
or a see-saw or a hand when it shakes another hand
or a tendon or a ligament or a poem or a paper clip
or a pin or a rope or a wire

The butcher shop closes down
and cleans out its insides. Everything
goes: cleavers, cutting boards,
hooks. The smell of blood fades,
the ghosts, if any, clear.

For a few months it's only four white walls,
a small chair in a dim corner, and a light bulb
hanging from the ceiling.

We gaze through the front windows
coming home from parties
or night-school classes. It's the nothing
we are drawn to, a kind of snowfall-nothing
or those empty pages at the end of a novel.

A month later, the Dollar Store
moves in and fills the room with racks
of glittering key chains and baskets
of toy dinosaurs.

We look in there less;
it's still nothing, but a different kind.
I go in once to buy a broom, and another time
a dozen tea candles, even though
I had stepped inside for
something else.

the music chimes, the bicycle
climbs the hill, the clock releases
a bird. The streetlight blinks, goes night
day night day night. My bed
is a giant reset button I hold down
until morning. When the teeth
of the dream meet the teeth of the morning
I pour myself a cup of numbers in the kitchen.
Daydream a wheel inside a wheel. Daydream
children running from the shore with cupped
phosphorescence that dies out before
they reach us. Rushing back to do it again.
And I am a child running toward myself
and the teeth of the memory meet the teeth
of the day meet the clock, the highway, the heart.
Or the gears don't touch, just spin like ceiling fans.
What's a day? asks the sun. What's night?
asks the moon. Will you send me
that beautiful book about asteroids?
I want my life to change.

The parked car rolls down its windows. Out comes thin smoke, coughing, laughter and there are my friends in the nineteen nineties. Shoulders touching, bare feet on a dashboard. A highway billboard nearby promises affordable travel. Then the slats turn in unison and a movie announces it will blow your mind. Evan narrows his eyes and says, *Promise?* Alison tries to take pictures on her flashless disposable camera and they come out murky black when developed days later. Nothing was purchased tonight and nothing sold. Friends turn to acquaintances turn to strangers turn to dormant volcanoes in my chest. The billboard shuffles again and the new image promises that for the meantime you are good and real in their eyes. Then back to affordable travel, shark-free blue beaches, and the doubt returns. In the nineteen nineties the moon is a backlit bus-shelter ad with the poster removed, promising nothing and everything. Promise you'll stay the same means promise you'll change on a trajectory parallel to mine means we're bound to grow apart. Here is the final gratitude for that. What did I want to say to you all, ghosting back like this? Turn off the radio and sing instead. Oh, and take her hand. You know who. The one who needs it most.

We took the 601 into the city, double-clicking
catchphrases in raw throats, a beer bottle
rolling in pulses down the bus aisle. All the skulls
on all the hoodies in the Rock Shop
laughing at us on our arrival. Laughed back
from our own skulls. Being hustled
on the art gallery steps, smoking the oregano anyway,
smiles carved into our faces. Friends who appeared
like giants by our town's driftwood fires, now slapped
pale and diminished in this crowded light.

Asking for it, even. That monk's mud-puddle shove.
A night school that could teach me something about
night itself. It was slow education. My head
a Walkman that kept eating cassettes. For all I knew,
the glass office buildings were full of sorcerers
and dark arts. Missed the last bus home, wrote
a run-on sentence in my notebook, watched
it slink off the page and scribble darkly
through the streets. Years later,

I'll be living here, still editing that sentence, my old bicycle
winding past cherry trees toward the public library,
or for coffee with a friend. I'll cycle through
whole neighbourhoods I didn't know existed back then,
roads with islands of traffic-calming circular gardens, tulips
coming up bright and swordless in the spring air.

Watching the hooded boy carrying his skateboard and a bouquet of flowers down a suburban street, quarter past lavender. He's looking down the whole time, headphones covering his ears, holding this fireworkishly luminous thing at a precise distance away from himself. Brings it closer to his body when the wind picks up.

Spicy orange nasturtiums on the cutting board and the child makes a show of gnashing one with her teeth.

A scientist dips a red rose into a tank of liquid nitrogen before dropping the rose to shatter on the tile floor. Then he moves onto other things.

A man phones a flower delivery service from his office. When asked how many roses he falters: A dozen? Two dozen? Fifty? A hundred? Six wheelbarrows full? A truck full? Roses piled high enough to cause a traffic obstruction in front of her house?

Suggestions to Management #17: A single orchid in every warehouse lunchroom. More in the ones that don't have windows.

The girl at the flower shop says she's against the use of specific flowers or specific colours of roses to signify only specific cultural occasions or moods, as it limits the rich possibilities of said flowers or colours to operate within other contexts and meanings.

Limping back to my bike, cherry blossoms on the slow turning front wheel.

Why not plant the flowers directly on the grave? Is it that their vitality seems to mock the dead? Do the cut ones show communion?

On the drunken walk home, I steal a dahlia as big as my face. Trying to cut through the tough stem with my fingernail, wondering if I should carry a switchblade for instances such as this.

I ask the girl at the coffee shop for a pen to borrow and she gives me one with a large fake rose (complete with glitter and acrylic dewdrops) attached to it—a theft deterrent. I have to tilt my head to see what my hand is writing.

I almost bring it home to you.

Every spring when the trees are in full blossom I have this thought: *That must hurt.* And then the thought that always follows: *Why would anyone think that?*

She's out into the late dusk, editing the garden.

She calls me over to smell something tiny and white growing over a neighbour's gate, makes me get my face right up and breathe deep that heart-aching, knee-weakening, circuit-frying, synaesthesia-inducing scent.

Half past lavender, the sky revealing its sweet limits.

He collects his friends' broken Walkmans
and builds a flying machine out of them. Straps in
and launches from his rooftop in the fading light,
just after the crows have passed. These are the controls:
rewind, fast-forward, play and stop. All other variables
are left to the music, old mixes from friends. One of the tape's
ribbon is wrinkled in places from a recent unspooling.
It murmurs and crackles, but it still lifts the rickety machine.
Another tape contains, in the last empty minutes, rainfall,
a train in the distance. Someone says something he strains
to hear. At this particular height, the landscape is toy-like,
a miniature model, despite what all hell
he has been through down there. The blue eyes
of backyard swimming pools. A soccer field
like a green diary, locked. What all hell.
He coasts for a while in silence just above the streetlights
after the last tape clicks to its end. Lifted by something
approaching grace.

Daniel took an axe to a young fir tree in the grove
behind the dance school. Trevor immersed himself
in a book on the elements of typography. Clive smashed
his mother's favourite vase and spent the next week
painstakingly gluing the pieces back together. Rob spent
all his free time at the gym, building a coat of muscle
around his slender frame. Michael gazed at his drink
as if it were a jar of dimly glowing fireflies. Dean listened to
an old murder ballad for an entire night, becoming
more and more gentle with each repeat. Adam began
his fight for the preservation of the bird habitat in
his community. Spencer bought a beautiful motorcycle
that spoke like a lion. Billy gave up smoking. Patrick started.
David went on a pilgrimage, the Camino de Santiago.
Ian didn't feel anything until he saw the destroyed fir tree
in the grove behind the dance school. Then he gasped
her name.

A rooftop will do in a town
with no cliffs. A Friday night
with cheap Merlot and a cheaper
radio will do. The wind
stirs, faint skunk then honeysuckle.
She tucks her arms and head into
the front of her T-shirt to light
the joint. I picture a cloud of smoke
between her small breasts.
Her shirt, stretched and faded,
says *Save the Tigers* across it. But
there are no more tigers left
on this earth. We smoke on the edge
of the roof, sneakers dangling. Crackling
music from a time and place
we've never been. It will do. The day's
heat still holds to the shingles.
She's lying on her back, looking up,
saving tigers. *Don't tell her,* repeats
in my goddamn head. Don't tell her.

Woke up, made some calls, James came over, we drew the dark
curtains closed, smoked up and played video games.
He destroyed me then I destroyed him then he destroyed me.
And then he destroyed me again. Sandra called and talked to James
on the phone while I tried to read the newspaper
and before hanging up he said, *Take care, baby* real small
and quiet. Translation: *You destroy me.* He put on that album
and it was like icebergs calving into the sea. I couldn't understand
most of the newspaper. My little sister Alexis
ran into the room dressed as a ladybug and hugged my arm
and her pipe-cleaner antennae brushed my cheek
and it sort of destroyed me. James and I smoked another one
and played another game. This time we were both destroyed
by bear-like creatures that came out of nowhere. They fed on us
right there in the game's misted forest. Total destruction
and the screen faded to black and I started to feel faint
so I got up and stepped over to the window, drew the curtains
in one fast movement and the sunlight tore right through me
and James said, *What?* and I just stood there awhile looking
at the red leaves coming off the trees and waited for the light
to finish what it had started.

WHITE NOISE GENERATOR
for Amanda Todd

The autumn air feels guilt, the trees feel guilt, the cables and the pixels, the birds and the ditch. A tornado forms, tries to suck a ghost back down from its slow lift. Fails, then roars through the town, then the next town. Makes a point to hit every billboard on the way.

Horses run through seafoam, white horses running through a calendar. The cold chemical smell of a permanent marker squeaking over rectangles of paper. A mood ring on her hand rotating through the spectrum. All the strength needed in the narration, the thorn that digs deeper with the telling. What happened and is happening and the strength needed still.

Friend request like a conch shell left on your doorstep. Friend request like devil-horning every face in my old yearbook while on the phone into the wee hours. Friend request like would you like to see the portal I found in the school's darkroom? Friend request like let's cover ourselves in wet leaves and mud before math class. Friend request like I'll be your white noise generator.

An ocean is a good listener. An ocean works the teen suicide hotline 24-7. A conch shell (stay with me) is a telephone.

Friend request like a poem typed in an empty chat room at the end of the night. Friend request like I got a rooftop, a joint and a handful of stars with your name on it. Friend request like what is difficult is what is necessary is what is actually listening to another human speaking.

Picture a pear tree in the middle of a wasteland where the pear tree is you and the wasteland is the comments section.

Never interrupt a girl while she is trying to draw a horse. Never laugh when she whisper-sings under her breath walking across the soccer field. She may be summoning dragons, she may be summoning them against you.

Flashcards held in front of a window. Another then another. Trust and we shall be the receiver; love and we shall be the amplifier—until the amplifier short circuits, the windows blow out and silence splashes everywhere.

When I eat this burger, this popular fast food cheeseburger,
alone in the driver's seat, parked by a river,

the knowledge that there are thousands, maybe tens
of thousands, experiencing this identical flavour
and texture at this precise time,

brings me (don't laugh) comfort. That I don't really enjoy
the meal is not important. I keep from turning on
the radio, given the music that I fear haunts it.

Pixels of moonlight on the slow-moving water.
Lines on the grid I should not snap to, but do every time.

Something dark and knowing inside me always seems to win.

*

Bumper stickers:

My other car will carry me beyond this mortal world.

My other car does not compromise other people's lives.

My other car's glovebox is full of wild sage.

*

I dreamed I invented a second horn-sound for a car
meant to communicate *Sorry*.

I dreamed I worked at a factory where they made arrow signs
for directions on roads and highways. Arrows coming down

conveyor belts, stacked in boxes, rejects piled in a garbage bin,
pointing in all directions. I dreamed

I crowd-surfed my way home, but don't remember
any people or music, just the feeling of the hands. I woke up

(okay, you can laugh) in tears. Now,

washing the miserable meal down with Coca-Cola, trying to feel
each of the bubbles burst on my tongue. Each complete
as the earth. Small and spherical

in the sweet dark that always seems to win.

Let leaping embers burn through the open journal,
the shoes, the army surplus jacket, the skin.

Let the driftwood fire converse
with something in your chest
as if you weren't there. Let it continue

until the police come down and instruct you
to kick sand over the flames. And before that

someone always hefts a log, burning at one end,
into the low tide. It hisses darkly. Nobody knows
what it means, but it's not like we are in the business

of meaning things. You take off your grey-green jacket
and offer it to a shivering girl but she shakes her head.

You set the jacket down and it crawls into the ocean,
starts swimming out. Swims back an hour later, dripping
and wiser.

What we feared: spiders, snakes, ourselves, drowning,
embarrassment, girls, ourselves. A chord fumbled
at a crucial moment, killing the song.

Later outside a 7-Eleven a man says, *Watch out
for the bombs tonight* and I don't get it.
Later, in a car window reflection,

I do. We pretend we are so gentle, so gentle
we are not capable of a fist in a face,
until we are, and then we are

frightened by our own wolf eyes in mirrors,
shivering at a breakfast table in the early dawn
after the long what-have-I-done night.

Your jacket still smells of driftwood smoke
after a few washes. Even after
you get it together, move out, get a job

wearing a staticky headset, receiving
calls from strangers miles away.

Let the ember burn through.
Set your jacket down and it crawls
into the ocean and doesn't come back.
Let it stay there. In her way,

she's wearing it and while
she's wearing it, thinking of you.

Cross-legged on his bed reading something in the dim curtained evening. Glow of standby lights on all the machines. A metallic geometry case beside him on the bed.

Streetlight-hunch. Eyes rubbed with roses.

A son assembles a cloud, furthers his education.

A head does what, says the heart. A head turns, half-static half-music, an antenna in a gale.

Names of girls on a few planets on his solar system poster. But don't. Don't ask.

A son takes a walk for a walk's sake, a nightwalk, for night's sake. Beatboxes past houses. Hushed snares, roof-of-the-mouth clicks, leaf-rustle, wind chimes.

To be lit up, attentive and caring. As if asking fireflies in a field to stay on all at once. While the field attends to its scared and lost.

A heart does what, says the head. A heart transmits.

I reached into a coat and found a marble that led to you. That led to a world that led to a world where I stood with a skull-patched coat, a blue marble.

Could have grown up, yes. Could have made sense. But I'd have forgotten the songs, lost my levitation powers. Though I guess I lost them anyway.

There was the thought and there was the turn toward another thought. What mattered was not so much the thoughts themselves but the beauty of the turn, the white flowers that grew along the curve, their sudden blossoming and disappearing.

A gentle high-voiced son waiting under a streetlight. A goodnighting. Watch him turn the corner with a hooded friend and disappear into a grove of trees.

To be watched over by the forces therein.

jamessmokingmarijuanathroughapotatopipe.jpg

lightsmearedghostsonthegreencouch.jpg

thiskidnobodyknowswearingthepuffiestjacketeverandweall callhimlittlelionwhichheseemstolike.jpg

marysshouldershighintheroom.jpg

jakeplayingwishyouwerehereonmyguitarforthethousandth timeandallofusreallywanthimtostop.jpg

storytellinginthegreenhouse.jpg

thisiswhyevelynleft.jpg

sunsetpasthepowerlines.jpg

postsunsetcrowsflyingeastward.jpg

someoneborrowedmycameraandtookpicturesofmysiamese fightingfish6of18.jpg

thisamazingspreadoffoodmycuprunnethoveretcetc.jpg

headphonesonadeerskull.jpg

damieninmidair.jpg

mydogcodysleepingonthebalconysurroundedbylonglegsgoing
upforever.jpg

aliciagivesthislookthatalwaysmakesmewonderifthiswillbethe
lastpictureofher.jpg

colininaskirtsweepingbeerbottleglass.jpg

FOR A NEIGHBOURHOOD

A flower delivery driver
is lost in a bad neighbourhood.

The moon is full
and his van is full
of roses.

Take a breath,
says the moon.

Even if the roses
end up in the wrong hands

they'll be in the right hands.

DUST

You're sneezing because you're emptying the house,
you're moving, you're packing and moving,
you're moving things you have not touched,
not looked upon since your last move,
the keepsakes that kept to themselves, that kept still
as dust rained on them, from them,
the dust circles the room, you're leaking
and sneezing, your lungs intake air, force it
out through your mouth and nose, your arm
jerks to cover, your sleeve damp, your eyes red,
the skin around your nostrils red,
you're sweating and itching, the dust sticks
to your forehead, the sunlight sticks
to the dust, the house lets go of the home,
the home turns back into the house
you first staggered into, carrying boxes
of your possessions, sneezing, sneezing.

AFTER HOURS AT THE CENTRE FOR DIALOGUE
for David Foster Wallace

The janitor pulls the string of the vertical blinds
of the window that looks out onto a bustling
Friday night. The blinds rotate in unison, the light
sliced thinner. His new vacuum has the softest
roar he has ever heard a vacuum make. A D-minor
whisper. There are some phrases around in the room,
on posters and sticky notes: *Trust is the byproduct*
of respect, and *Cerebral discussions often stalemate.*
Move it into your body, and new realizations
become possible. He moves a damp cloth
over window ledges. Drags the mop
in figure eights over the smooth granite tile
of the lobby, noticing the evaporation
that has already begun where he started.
Be aware of non-verbal messages.
To listen well, you must be fully present
and engaged. Someone has left a cup of water
on a desk and he pours it into the soil
of a potted plant on another desk. He resets
the chairs around the boardroom table,
making sure to leave a particular amount
of space between the back of the chair
and the table edge, promoting a sense of welcome.
Sprays the washroom mirrors with window cleaner
and then buffers with newspaper. He inspects
the mirror for dirt or prints, and catches
the reflection of his own eyes. They look

tired and concerned. He eases his expression
to a more neutral one and senses himself
becoming calmer before it.

Small unidentifiable noises hushcrackle
over my headset.

In neighbouring cubicles other humans, sleep deprived
and coffee-buzzed, workflow through their daydreams.

Somewhere, Alabama. A woman is shopping online for gifts
and her afternoon is *this close* to being ruined. The next few
minutes on the phone with me will determine the outcome.

Little beeps could be small animals,
whirrs, cats in the grass.

I will meet your frustration, show I empathize
and outline possible solutions. I will diffuse tension
with cadence and tone. Eyes closed and fingers
in circular motions at my temple.

You could ask me about the weather. You might still.

Other figures in separate rooms listen in, error-check,
highlight where I have deviated too far from the script.

Quality, assurance. Our voices archived indefinitely.

Somewhere, Alabama. A dog barks, a man shouts.

Click that. Tell me what you see. Okay, good.

Small noises, fine-print hiss. Flowers
shipped, inexplicably, across landforms.

We can deviate from the script if it makes your experience
a more positive one, Alabama.

Weather? It is snowing here. I'm glad you asked because
I've been wanting to say that. *It's snowing*. I'd hold my headpiece
out the window, but the windows here, though wide and tall,
don't open.

What would we be listening for, anyway?

If strangers have asked you to slow down at least four
or five times this week, maybe they are right—consider
that you are wrong, and spend your evening learning

some new chords. Spend what you possess in great quantities
and does not destroy. You were wrong at the school
and wrong at the bicycle repair shop and wrong

in your comments on the internet. Accept it like a sudden rain,
like an unexpected note that worries the chord
into a more radiant one. Night flowers open with ease

in the politician's garden. White lion statues lift a paw as if asking
to remove a thorn. If strangers have asked you to slow down
when it seemed that you were standing still

as everything blurred past. If you, in the hot exhaust, try to cool.
Breathe in the night air, begin to pearl the irritant. A little moon
you can pocket, keep to remind.

AN ACHE IN THE KNOT

if there's a shortness in the breath of the lungs
if there's an ache in the muscles of the arm

if there's a knot in the shoulder and a soreness
in the throat if there's a redness in the eye

and a twitch in the lid if there's heat in the forehead
or sweat in the sheets if there's weakness in the knees

or a hunger in the gut if a clutch of the fist
a ringing in the ear a chill to the touch or a sprain

of the wrist a shock to an elbow a swell in the bruise
a cut in the skin a skip in the heart if there's love

in the inhale or love in the exhale if we are making amends
if there's a mending of the bodies that rend

if we tend to each other in the dimming room
if there is an ache in the knot undone

THE MORNING AFTER NIGHT

I listened to the noises the house made,
catalogued the sounds and slept.

Invented some things while asleep
and upon waking, destroyed them.

I watched tiny bits of dust suspended in the lit air,
registered the absence, and gathered what I had.

Drifting ice sheets, torn versions of last night's manifesto,
scatter the floor.

The orange gets better reception after it is peeled.
The strangest song always makes sense
before the day's machinery whirrs alive.

If you think flowers are silent you haven't heard them make love,
that soft buzzing in the garden.

And so now, now you have.

The last assembly instruction is always you reading this.
A machine that rarely functions, but could never
without you.

THE SKY ABOVE THE STADIUM

Outside the stadium, fathers in parked cars
feel the deep rumble from their children's imagination.

Two nervous women hand out flyers of Bible verses.
Half of them are redistributed by the wind
swirl with bus tickets, receipts, crisp leaves.

Who will inherit, what is inherited, what do we do
with what we receive.

A few songs in, the ticket scalpers one by one
descend a staircase down
to the dark centre of the earth.

The deep rumble. The ten thousand years.
The sweet sound.

Tattoos swim across the bodies of the girls.
Blessed are the wretched carried across
our sea of hands.

What is the sky doing above the stadium? Dusky,
flecked with brilliant pink and orange. Shocking

and strange and welcoming all winged,
screeching forms.

CAR GAME

Morning rush hour, a man stands on
the railing of a bridge in a white office shirt
studying the waves.

Someone in one of the many stuck cars
calls a radio station, explains what's going on,
and requests Van Halen's "Jump."

The DJ, after a chuckle,
plays the song (and when asked days later
if this was the right thing to do
says he'd do it again).

If you are breathing here in this poem
you are breathing new car interior. Roll down
the windows and there's exhaust,
a hint of ocean.

You are breathing the invisible particles
you read about in a book
that have entered and exited billions of chests
since the beginning of breath.

If the heart is the engine for love,
what are the lungs for?

And it is true, there is something funny
about the song request
the riffy optimism of the music
held against the grey
hard-to-look-in-the-eye moment
of the day.

Some turn it up, not making the connection:
they just like the song. It's got a good hook.

Many turn off their radios, kill
their engines.

Boats drift under the bridge, boaters in sunglasses
with life jackets and morning coffee.
A part of the white-shirted man's mind
is occupied with avoiding them in timing the fall.

There are seabirds in this poem
who have no idea what they are here for.

Breathe in the about-to-rain air.

Breathe in and imagine
the man as a child
learning to tie his shoelaces.

A child with a clear inner logic, arranging
stuffed toys on the shelf
above his bed.

A child imitating the shape
and movement of an airplane.

It's just a car game to play.
Something to pass the time.

Imagine the hard impact
against water. Then the give.

Your shirt flaps loose, a white flag.

You look down. There's an ocean
past your shoes.

You can smell the ocean. It smells of a million things.

You have to let go of something
to reach what you are trying to reach

what the people in their cars are trying to reach

what the concerned people who inch toward you
with their arms out and eyebrows high
are trying to reach

you must let go and fall
in one direction
or another

TRANSMITTER AND RECEIVER

A man stood outside our house with our dinner
because you were tired from the child
and I was tired from my shift at work
and neither of us wanted to cook and clean.
A man stood under our porch light
in a neighbourhood in East Vancouver
on a rainy evening near the beginning of summer,
his car idling in our driveway. I answered
the door in my housecoat, gave him my card,
pressed some numbers on a keypad;
transmitting it said, then *receiving.*
He handed me the warm boxes of pizza,
thanked me, I thanked him and he walked back
to his logo-painted car and drove away.
I put a few slices on white plates
and brought them to you in the living room
taking soft steps so as to not wake the baby.
We ate and watched nature documentaries.
A couple cans of IPA eased a knot in my shoulder.
We watched a bower bird construct an elaborate nest,
a giraffe stretch for high leaves, a storm cloud
form in time-lapse over a savannah.
And it felt strange to me not inviting him in
and introducing him to my family,
this man from Iran holding pizza boxes in one arm,
standing under a light fevered with moths
outside a stranger's house, we the tired strangers
with a new son. He must have known there was someone
sleeping by how I whispered at the door
and I must have known he knew
by how he whispered too.

AN ONLINE FRIEND DIES SOMEWHERE OUTSIDE THE INTERNET

Freezes, goes blue screen, shuts down. Dead pixel, dark.
Ghost echoes, lossy in the source code. Time zones away,
people who have actually shaken hands with my online friend
stand around a box of his remains. I'm left to click through data,
two-dimensional and without decay, in multiple windows.

Close all until I'm left by the one that renders birds, sky,
and keep-moving-nothing-to-see-here clouds. Nothing
to see here. I go for a walk to the edge of town, daydream
a closed-loop whirlwind in a field of tall grass.
Cast a rock into the dark old sea.

Melting glacier, to be honest, I only skimmed your letter.
Rising ocean, I poured all my savings into bad cinema.
Gathering storm, I did not consider the narrative
of my coffee beans. I settled on lazy automatics, I ate
the messenger animals.

Calving iceberg, you asked a beautiful question. I faltered.
Fevered sea, my blood thickens with jellyfish. Can I take
something for this? Can I use the heat of this
for any practical use? Approaching hurricane,

I am apologizing too late. They kept telling me to stay
in the moment. So here is the moment. I drove
a million cars down a million highways to clear my head.
I drove and drove, burning forest, I drove and drove
and drove and drove and drove.

POSSIBLEWOLF

We watch the sleeping newborn with disbelief
because, we think, she must

trust her surroundings enough to fall asleep there,
trust the swaying blinds, shards of light, the mobile

of origami cranes in slow twirl, the ticking clock,
the owl, the fox, the vase of yellow roses,

the textured ceiling, the shelf of books, all of which
she cannot comprehend. How could she? But there she is,

asleep on the bed, in the soft mouth of the world.
And us, Possiblewolf, Possiblebear, watching over her,

flickering. Transforming.

This ceiling, this frame, this room, these windows.
It is not so strange to be sad at the thought
that you are the only person you'll ever get to be.
But when you see your child or wife or father
or even a stranger sitting across from you,
across a table, or on a train, reading
or looking at something just outside
your field of view, and you think
that they are the only people they will ever
get to be—how much more surprising
to find yourself more sad, or within a deeper,
more complex emotion. Not because
you pity them, but because it allows you,
in that instance, to love them in a way
you rarely do. If love is to know self. If self
is to know other. How small those few seconds,
how wide. And in the particular case of your wife,
how miraculous it feels. That in this only life she has,
she called you into it. This ceiling, this frame,
this room, these windows.

A book where a mountain appears overnight next to a village and all the villagers are too afraid to climb it except for the animals and the children.

A book where your father and mother are planets and you are a moon orbiting each of them in turn and sometimes you comet away into space, a slight angle in your trajectory.

A book of the world that existed before you. A man's hat blows off in a gust of wind before you. A woman washes her face in a stream before you. A cat holds a goldfinch in its mouth before you.

A book on how to responsibly operate and maintain your alphabet.

A book that runs on solar power. Or runs on your mother playing the piano in the other room. Or on your own breathing. Or on your own eyes upon the pages.

A book that's folded into an origami crane. You don't want to open it up. No—you want to, but know it would never fold back into the same bird.

A book where no mention is made of money.

A book where the stars are reachable with an ordinary stepladder and the ocean is a postman who comes right up to your front gate and no mention is made of money.

A book about animals that are so kind they do not eat each other and live on sunlight and flowers in a meadow but they are always hungry and the book is small enough to fit in your chest pocket and the book is thick enough to absorb a bullet.

A book that explains the stages of the earth's water cycle in detail and what that teaches us about love.

A book about an elephant that wants to live at the bottom of the ocean and what that teaches us about love.

A dream dictionary which won't ever be read but whose pages are fed into the fireplace through the winter.

A book about you that I'm holding in my hands right now this late evening, pages blank as the moon sailing across the whole length of our window.

The descending two notes
that signal my cellphone needs recharging
imitate the chirp of a hungry baby bird.
You go *Awwh* when you hear it. And the sound
when I plug it into the wall
is a small, satisfied chirp. These design choices
were made in rooms with windows,
or without windows. I hear
there is a clearing in a park in this city
where one can hold out one's hand
and a bird will eventually land on it.
I have the precise GPS coordinates
somewhere. We walk the city together
while chameleons and seahorses,
bathed in afterlife-white glow,
try to sell us plans from bus-stop
advertisements. I'm worried about
how this will affect the nature documentaries
that already risk anthropomorphism.
I want a cellphone with fur that bristles.
Or changes colour like a bothered
octopus. I hope no one calls today.
But if you call I'll answer, because
of how your voice cuts through the noise
of the day, and how the noise that has
been building inside me diminishes,
a swarm of bees leaving the hive
toward flowers somewhere.

ACKNOWLEDGEMENTS

Previous versions of poems from this book have appeared in *Prism International*, *The Malahat Review*, *subTerrain Magazine*, *Poetry Is Dead*, *Quills*, *CV2*, *Echolocation*, *Forget Magazine*, *Papirmass* and the anthology *Alive at the Center: Contemporary Poems from the Pacific Northwest*.

This book-machine is set to transmit gratitude to all who have helped in its formation. There are so many individuals but I would like to explicitly thank the following:

Thank you to Rob Taylor and Jen Currin for being careful and attentive first readers.

Thank you to my mentors and teachers who challenged and encouraged me, especially Patrick Friesen, Rachel Rose and Jami Macarty.

Thank you to all the folks at the Writers' Trust and those involved with the Bronwen Wallace Award for Emerging Writers.

Thank you to Nicholas and Lindsay Bradford-Ewart for adapting my poem "After Lydia" into a stunning short film.

Thank you to my family for their love, support and patience, especially my parents Joseph Fernandes and Faye Carvaliho, and my in-laws Margaret Cornish and Andrea Mann.

Thank you to my friends and peers, past and present, faraway and near, for keeping me on this earth.

Thank you to everyone at Nightwood Editions and Harbour Publishing especially Grace Cheung, Grace Lane, my excellent editor Silas White and Carleton Wilson who designed the beautiful cover.

Thank you to my wife Megan and my son Leith for continuously opening up my heart.

Raoul Fernandes has been writing poetry since childhood, and is involved in both online and offline writing communities. He completed the Writer's Studio at Simon Fraser University in 2009. He was a finalist for the 2010 Bronwen Wallace Award for Emerging Writers. He lives and writes in Vancouver, BC, where he also composes electronic music under the moniker Goodnight Streetlight.

PHOTO: ERNST SCHNEIDER